Izzy Hayden for Salt Lick Produc
in association with Neil McPher:
presents

The world premiere

C000184168

BACON

by Sophie Swithinbank

First performance at the Finborough Theatre: Tuesday, 1 March 2022

Bacon was originally developed by Soho Theatre and was the winner of the
Tony Craze Award.

This production has been supported by Soho Theatre.

BACON

by Sophie Swithinbank

Cast in order of speaking

Mark	**Corey Montague-Sholay**
Darren	**William Robinson**

The action takes place in West London. The present.

The approximate running time is 70 minutes.

There will be no interval.

Director	**Matthew Iliffe**
Set and Costume Designer	**Natalie Johnson**
Lighting Designer	**Ryan Joseph Stafford**
Sound Designer	**Mwen**
Intimacy Director	**Jess Tucker Boyd**
Casting Consultant	**Nadine Rennie**
Stage Manager	**Jessica McGarry**
Producer	**Izzy Hayden**
Associate Producer	**Alan Mackintosh**
Assistant Producer	**Iona Bremner**

PLEASE BE CONSIDERATE OF OTHERS AND WEAR A FACE COVERING FULLY COVERING YOUR MOUTH AND NOSE FOR THE DURATION OF THE PERFORMANCE.

Please see front of house notices or ask an usher for an exact running time.

Please turn your mobile phones off – the light they emit can also be distracting.

Our patrons are respectfully reminded that, in this intimate theatre, any noise such as the rustling of programmes, food packaging or talking may distract the actors and your fellow audience members.

We regret there is no admittance or readmittance to the auditorium whilst the performance is in progress.

Corey Montague-Sholay | Mark

Trained at Bristol Old Vic Theatre School.

Theatre includes *Wendy & Peter Pan* (Leeds Playhouse), *She Stoops to Conquer* and *As You Like It* (Guildford Shakespeare Company), *The Whip* and *King John* (Royal Shakespeare Company), *This Island's Mine* (King's Head Theatre), *Henry V* (Shakespeare at The Tobacco Factory), *The Enchanted* (The Bunker), *Normal* (Rift Theatre at Styx), *Snow White* (Sixteenfeet Productions at Brixton East), *The Hotel Cerise* (Theatre Royal Stratford East), *Little Revolution* and *ICU* (Almeida Theatre) and *Carpe Diem* (National Theatre).

Short film includes *Kite Strings, Angry Face, Callum, Our Night* and *Home*.

William Robinson | Darren

Trained at LAMDA.

Theatre includes *Romeo and Juliet* (National Tour) and *Target Man* (King's Head Theatre). Theatre whilst training includes *Three Days in the Country, The Two Gentlemen of Verona, Country Music* and *In Arabia We'd All Be Kings*.

Short film includes *Queens* and *Femme*.

Television includes *Masters of the Air* and *Cuffs*.

Sophie Swithinbank | Playwright

Bacon won the Soho Theatre's Tony Craze Award, and is currently in development for a television adaptation with NBCUniversal.

Her other plays include *Circle Game* (Oxford School of Drama and Southwark Playhouse), *Even In Arcadia* (longlisted for the Verity Bargate Award), *The Fellowship* (Picturedrome, University of Northampton), *Where There Is Smoke* (National Theatre Learning), *Come Inside* (Bush Theatre) and *The Superhero* (Lyric Theatre, Hammersmith).

Matthew Iliffe | Director

Productions at the Finborough Theatre include *The Niceties, Maggie May* and *Geography of Fire/La Furie et sa Géographie* as part of *Vibrant 2019 – A Festival of Finborough Playwrights*.

Matthew graduated from the University of Bristol with a first-class honours degree in Theatre and Performance Studies, and trained on the Stonecrabs Young Directors Programme.

Theatre includes *Four Play* (Above The Stag Theatre) and *The Burnt Part Boys* (Park Theatre).

Theatre as an Assistant Director includes *A Midsummer Night's Dream* (Changeling Theatre Company), *Romeo and Juliet* (Insane Root Theatre Company) and *Brass* (Hackney Empire).

Theatre as Associate Director includes *Musik* (Leicester Square Theatre).

Natalie Johnson | Set and Costume Designer

Trained at The Liverpool Institute for Performing Arts and was awarded the Liverpool Everyman and Playhouse Prize for Stage Design in 2017.

Theatre includes *Very Special Guest Star* (Omnibus Theatre), *Flinch* (National Tour), *Dumbledore Is So Gay, Catching Comets, The Rage of Narcissus* (Pleasance London), *39 and Counting* (Park Theatre), *John & Jen* (Southwark Playhouse), *Macbeth* (Theatre Peckham), *The Shadow* (HOME Manchester), *Tick... Tick... Boom!* (Bridge House Theatre), *Bluebeard* (Alphabetti Theatre), *Twelfth Night* (Bridge House Theatre and Globe Neuss, Germany), *Mydidae, Putting It Together, The Wasp* (Hope Mill Theatre, Manchester), *Striking 12* (Union Theatre), *Eris* (The Bunker), *To Anyone Who Listens* (Hen and Chickens Theatre), and *Othello* (Liverpool Everyman).

Theatre as Associate Designer includes *Last Easter* (Orange Tree Theatre, Richmond), *Everything Is Absolutely Fine* (The Lowry, Salford) and *Forgotten* (Arcola Theatre and Theatre Royal Plymouth).

Ryan Joseph Stafford | Lighting Designer

Productions at the Finborough Theatre include *Not Quite Jerusalem* and *The Wind of Heaven.*

Trained at Rose Bruford College and is the recipient of the Michael Northern Award for Excellence in Lighting Design from the Association of Lighting Designers.

Theatre includes *Isla, Curtain Up* (Clwyd Theatr Cymru), *Shades of Blue, NYDC X Russell Maliphant* (Sadler's Wells), *Left from Write* (Norwegian National Ballet II, Royal Opera House, Covent Garden, and European Tour), *Cyrano de Bergerac, Easy Virtue* (Watermill Theatre, Newbury), *The Island* (National Tour), *Cardiff Boy* (The Other Room, Cardiff) and *The Secret Lives of Baba Segi's Wives* (Arcola Theatre).

Mwen | Sound Designer

Mwen is a Sound Designer, Artist, Producer, Composer and DJ. Their creative practice blends the worlds of music technology, electronic music, live sound and performance. Mwen's compositions and productions have received airplay on BBCR1, BBCR6, XFM, NTS, Rinse FM and been supported by DJs including Rob da Bank, Mary Anne Hobbs and Tom Robinson and synced to TV and fashion film.

Theatre includes *Nightclubbing* (National and European Tour), *The Mob Reformers* (Lyric Theatre, Hammersmith), *My Name is My Own* (Southbank Centre), *I am [NOT] Kanye West* (The Bunker), *Tiger Mum* (Soho Theatre), *Voice It* (National Theatre Studio), *Winners* (Wardrobe Theatre) and *Straight White Men* (Southwark Playhouse).

Jess Tucker Boyd | Intimacy Director

Jess is a Senior Lecturer on the Acting for Contemporary and Devised Performance at the University of Northampton and Artistic Associate at the King's Head Theatre. She is Movement Director and Co-Director for The Alchemist Theatre Company, and is also a performer and is a published poet.

Movement Direction includes *Katzenmusik* (Royal Court Theatre), *BU21* (Trafalgar Studios), *Coming Clean* (King's Head Theatre), *Jelly Beans* (Theatre503), *Moormaid* (Arcola Theatre), *A Gym Thing* (Pleasance London) and *Gutted* (Marlowe Theatre, Canterbury).

Intimacy Coordination includes *Missing Julie* (Clwyd Theatr Cymru) and *Faustus: That Damned Woman* (Lyric Theatre, Hammersmith), and, for television, *I Hate Suzy* and *Dangerous Liaisons*.

Jessica McGarry | Stage Manager

Trained in MA Stage and Event Management at the Royal Welsh College of Music and Drama.

Theatre includes *Snow White and the Seven Dwarfs* (Bristol Hippodrome), *Nightmare Scenario* (Riverfront Studio Newport) and *Spellz* (National Tour).

Theatre whilst training includes *Wife*, *The Threepenny Opera* (Richard Burton Theatre) and *Statements After An Arrest Under The Immorality Act* (Sherman Studio).

Izzy Hayden | Producer

Theatre includes *Amphibian* (King's Head Theatre) and *The Lesson* (Southwark Playhouse and National Tour).

Theatre as Assistant Producer includes *Bobby and Amy* (National Tour).

Alan Mackintosh | Associate Producer

Alan is a Scotland-based independent producer, production accountant and founder of ALMACK Productions.

Iona Bremner | Assistant Producer

Iona graduated with a first-class degree in Theatre Studies and Film and Television Studies from the University of Glasgow, and is currently completing an MA in Creative Producing at the Royal Central School of Speech and Drama.

Production Acknowledgements

Production Consultant	**Tuyết Vân Huỳnh**
Artwork Modelling	**Alex Britt and Sam Craig**
Artwork Photography	**Darius Shu**
Dramaturgical Support	**David Luff**
Early Development	**Phoebe Ladenburg**

FINBOROUGH THEATRE

Founded in 1980, the multi-award-winning Finborough Theatre presents plays and music theatre, concentrated exclusively on vibrant new writing and unique rediscoveries from the 19th and 20th centuries, both in our 154-year-old home and online through our #FinboroughFrontier digital initiative.

Our programme is unique – we never present work that has been seen anywhere in London during the last 25 years. Behind the scenes, we continue to discover and develop a new generation of theatre makers.

Despite remaining completely unsubsidised, the Finborough Theatre has an unparalleled track record for attracting the finest talent who go on to become leading voices in British theatre. Under Artistic Director Neil McPherson, it has discovered some of the UK's most exciting new playwrights including Laura Wade, James Graham, Mike Bartlett, Jack Thorne, Nicholas de Jongh and Anders Lustgarten, and directors including Tamara Harvey, Robert Hastie, Blanche McIntyre, Kate Wasserberg and Sam Yates.

Artists working at the theatre in the 1980s included Clive Barker, Rory Bremner, Nica Burns, Kathy Burke, Ken Campbell, Jane Horrocks and Claire Dowie. In the 1990s, the Finborough Theatre first became known for new writing including Naomi Wallace's first play *The War Boys*, Rachel Weisz in David Farr's *Neville Southall's Washbag*, four plays by Anthony Neilson including *Penetrator* and *The Censor*, both of which transferred to the Royal Court Theatre, and new plays by Richard Bean, Lucinda Coxon, David Eldridge and Tony Marchant. New writing development included the premieres of modern classics such as Mark Ravenhill's *Shopping and F***king*, Conor McPherson's *This Lime Tree Bower*, Naomi Wallace's *Slaughter City* and Martin McDonagh's *The Pillowman*.

Since 2000, new British plays have included Laura Wade's London debut *Young Emma*, commissioned for the Finborough Theatre, James Graham's *Albert's Boy* with Victor Spinetti, Sarah Grochala's *S27*, Athena Stevens' *Schism* which was nominated for an Olivier Award, and West End transfers for Joy Wilkinson's *Fair*, Nicholas de Jongh's *Plague Over England*, Jack Thorne's *Fanny and Faggot*, Neil McPherson's Olivier Award nominated *It Is Easy To Be Dead*, and Dawn King's *Foxfinder*.

UK premieres of foreign plays have included plays by Brad Fraser, Lanford Wilson, Larry Kramer, Tennessee Williams, Suzan-Lori Parks, Jordan Tannahill, the English premieres of two Scots language classics by Robert McLellan, and West End transfers for Frank McGuinness' *Gates of Gold* with William Gaunt and John Bennett, and Craig Higginson's *Dream of the Dog* with Dame Janet Suzman.

Rediscoveries of neglected work – most commissioned by the Finborough Theatre – have included the first London revivals of Rolf Hochhuth's *Soldiers* and *The Representative*, both parts of Keith Dewhurst's *Lark Rise to Candleford*, *Etta Jenks* with Clarke Peters and Daniela Nardini, Noël Coward's first play *The Rat Trap*, Lennox Robinson's *Drama at Inish* with Celia Imrie and Paul O'Grady, Emlyn Williams' *Accolade*, and John Van Druten's *London Wall* (both of which transferred to St James' Theatre), and J. B. Priestley's *Cornelius* which transferred to a sell-out Off Broadway run in New York City.

Music Theatre has included the new (premieres from Craig Adams, Grant Olding, Charles Miller, Michael John LaChuisa, Adam Guettel, Andrew Lippa, Paul Scott Goodman, and Adam Gwon's *Ordinary Days* which transferred to the West End) and the old (the UK premiere of Rodgers and Hammerstein's *State Fair* which also transferred to the West End), and the acclaimed 'Celebrating British Music Theatre' series.

The Finborough Theatre won the 2020 London Pub Theatres Pub Theatre of the Year Award, *The Stage* Fringe Theatre of the Year Award in 2011, *London Theatre Reviews*' Empty Space Peter Brook Award in 2010 and 2012, swept the board with eight awards at the 2012 OffWestEnd Awards, and was nominated for an Olivier Award in 2017 and 2019. Artistic Director Neil McPherson was awarded the Critics' Circle Special Award for Services to Theatre in 2019. It is the only unsubsidised theatre ever to be awarded the Channel 4 Playwrights Scheme bursary eleven times.

www.finboroughtheatre.co.uk

Mailing
Email admin@finboroughtheatre.co.uk or give your details to our Box Office staff to join our free email list.

Playscripts
Many of the Finborough Theatre's plays have been published and are on sale from our website.

Local History
The Finborough Theatre's local history website is online at
www.earlscourtlocalhistory.co.uk

On Social Media
www.facebook.com/FinboroughTheatre
www.twitter.com/finborough
www.instagram.com/finboroughtheatre
www.youtube.com/user/finboroughtheatre

Friends

The Finborough Theatre is a registered charity. We receive no public funding, and rely solely on the support of our audiences. Please do consider supporting us by becoming a member of our Friends of the Finborough Theatre scheme. There are four categories of Friends, each offering a wide range of benefits.

Richard Tauber Friends – David and Melanie Alpers. James Baer. Nancy Balaban. David Barnes. Mike Bartlett. Letizia Belucci. Kate Beswick. Simon Bolland. Jamie Brookes. Malcolm Cammack. James Carroll. Denis Crapnell. Michael Diamond. Peter Dudas. Richard Dyer. Catrin Evans. Deirdre Feehan. Jeff Fergus. Stuart Ffoulkes. Lisa Forrell. Anne Foster. Patrick Foster. Julia Gallop. Nancy Goldring. Julian Goodwin. Judith Gunton. David Hammond. Mary Hickson. Christine Hoenigs. Laurence Humphreys-Davies. Damien Hyland. Richard Jackson. Liz Jones. Paul and Lindsay Kennedy. Martin and Wendy Kramer. Alex Laird. Georgina and Dale Lang. John Lawson. Emilia Leese. Maurice Lewendon. Toinette Lewendon. Frederick Lock. Harry MacAuslan. Rebecca Maltby. Kathryn McDowall. Susannah Meadway. Ghazell Mitchell. Graham Orpwood. Frederick Pyne. Annette Riddle. Elaine and Fred Rizzo. Chris Robinson. John Schmor. L Schulz. Jennifer Sharp. John Shea. Brian Smith. James Stitt. Caroline Thompson. Jan Topham. Lavinia Webb. Joan Weingarten and Bob Donnalley. Edwina D Wilcox. John Wilkes. Steven Williams. Jonathan Woods. Sylvia Young.

William Terriss Friends – Paul Guinery. Janet and Leo Liebster. Ros and Alan Haigh. Stephen Harper. Robert Rooney.

Adelaide Neilson Friends – Charles Glanville. Philip G Hooker.

Smoking is not permitted in the auditorium and the use of cameras and recording equipment is strictly prohibited.

PLEASE BE CONSIDERATE OF OTHERS, AND WEAR A FACE COVERING FULLY COVERING YOUR MOUTH AND NOSE FOR THE DURATION OF THE PERFORMANCE.

In accordance with the requirements of the Royal Borough of Kensington and Chelsea:

1. The public may leave at the end of the performance by all doors and such doors must at that time be kept open.

2. All gangways, corridors, staircases and external passageways intended for exit shall be left entirely free from obstruction whether permanent or temporary.

3. Persons shall not be permitted to stand or sit in any of the gangways intercepting the seating or to sit in any of the other gangways.

BACON

Sophie Swithinbank

Characters

MARK
DARREN

Characters played by Mark and Darren:
TEACHER
BLAIZE
RYAN
McDONALD'S EMPLOYEE
MARK'S MUM
DARREN'S DAD
HEADTEACHER

Design

The stage is reminiscent of a sad playground. This apparatus
should take up most of the space and be used in every scene.

Note on the Text

(/) Indicates an interruption.

(,) Indicates a beat.

Words in columns indicate a
split scene.

> They cannot see or hear each
> other, but their thoughts may
> sometimes connect.

*This text went to press before the end of rehearsals and so may
differ slightly from the play as performed.*

One

Now.

MARK. This is my story

And I've never told anyone before so. Don't interrupt. If that's okay. And don't ask questions because I don't have any answers so I might just stop telling it.

And you won't want that. (*Little smile.*) You won't want me to stop once I've started.

The reason I'm telling you now yeah, is because

he's here.

A bell tinkles, and a light reveals that DARREN *has been there since the beginning, sitting at the highest point of the climbing frame.*

He's here now. In the café. And, well, it's not just my story.

It's his story too.

Two

Four years earlier.

St Michael's School, Isleworth, London. Break time. MARK *is in the canteen.* DARREN *is behind the sports hall. They are in Year 10.*

MARK. It's the first day of
term and I think he sees me
before I see him. In fact, he
definitely sees me before I

see him. Because in form time, when I look up, he's looking right at me. I / swear.

Can't quite figure it out. He's looking at me and it's like he knows me. Do you ever get that?

MARK *takes a slurp of juice.*

I can feel his eyes on me. And that side of my face feels hot like the heat after a slap.

It's my first day here. My mum moved me to this school because… at my old school I… yeah…

Mum has not quite clocked that this school is worse. She thinks it's good coz it's Catholic but actually it's full of nutters who have probably got knives in their socks and guns in their pants.

MARK *looks around the canteen, warily.*

DARREN. Swear down my form group this year are shit man and the teacher's a massive –

DARREN *looks around to check the coast is clear, then lights a cigarette.*

Finks she can control me innit, this new teacher, man.

She's trying to get us all to fill out these fucking forms. These Good Behaviour Contracts and I'm like, I'm not signing anything. I want my lawyer. I walk straight out, clock / off for a quick cigarette.

DARREN *smokes.*

See just over there's a group of lads. Catholic lads, watching porn. Together. Right there. As if it's some kind of group activity.

The teacher spots DARREN.

Fuck's sake. She appears right in front of me, all frizzy hair and flappy skirts. (*As teacher; Northern Irish*.) 'How dare you walk out of my classroom Darren. I've just wasted twenty minutes of other students' learning time looking for you.'

Porn is not a group activity.

Is it?

DARREN *takes another toke of his cigarette*.

(*As teacher*.) 'Darren. This is school property. You can't smoke on school property.'

This is the 'sports hall'. It stinks like feet and sweat. We use it to play benchball when it's raining innit. Fucking benchball man. Literally not even a real sport.

I'm not in the mood for this frizzy woman so I stub my fag out on the sports hall wall and say, I didn't realise the school owned such shit property, sorry miss.

And then she goes – (*As teacher*.) 'You will be sorry, Darren.' And she

Got Geography in twenty
minutes and I want to
finish colour-coding my
population map of the
world. The biggest
countries on my population
map are China, India and
Bangladesh and I want to
colour them / red.

All the canteen tables are
full and I decide to find a
quiet place to finish my
map. I try the chapel but it's
locked. And I think, aren't
churches and stuff supposed
to be always open. To
welcome in the non-
believers and the homeless
and the hungry / and

Still haven't really got my
bearings…

I would really like to look
at the school map but that
would make me look lost
and that would mean
someone might come up to
me and talk to me or take
the piss.

stalks away, lanyard
swinging. I watch her go,
she's actually quite / hot.

Read somewhere that the
schools in this area have
got the least money of like
all the schools in London
or some shit innit. So that
explains it. That's why all
we have is a bench and a
ball. Fucking bench/ball.

I'm hungry and I fink
about going canteen but I
ain't got P.

(*Seeing* MARK, *lighting a
new cigarette*.) New lad is
wandering about like a
twat on his own. Twat.

I walk confidently towards the sports hall and... (*Sees* DARREN.) Shit.

They stare at each other for a moment.

MARK doesn't move.

It's the lad from my form group. He's leaning against the massive armadillo sports hall which makes him look small but in the form room with his eyes on me he seemed big...

Slowly, MARK *starts to move towards him.*

He's smoking a cigarette and wearing a Nike cap (both of which are not allowed). And maybe I should have a cigarette... it's my first day! Maybe I should just do something crazy and have a cigarette. With him. Maybe this is just what people do.

MARK *is close to* DARREN *now and they look at each other calmly in the eyes over the following:*

He's taller than me, and he's got pen all over his left hand which means he's probably right-handed. I can see that because I'm closer now and there's a little light somewhere. I'm closer now and

DARREN *nods* MARK *over.*

A light goes on.

,

,

DARREN. You're new innit?

MARK. Yeah just moved here from /

DARREN. Got no friends innit?

,

(*Louder.*) Got no fr– /

MARK. Well it's my first day.

DARREN. There's a lot of people in this school who will shit on you.

MARK (*aside*). I wonder if he is about to shit on me. I wonder if others will shit on me. I change the subject.

Did you see there's a group of people in the canteen watching porn?

DARREN (*laughing a bit*). Is it?

MARK (*joining the laugh*). Yeah.

DARREN *stops laughing.*

DARREN. Pervert.

MARK. What?

DARREN. Why you watching them for?

MARK. I wasn't, I…

DARREN. What's your name?

MARK. Mark.

DARREN. Mark.

MARK. What's yours?

,

DARREN. You a pervert, Mark?

MARK. No.

They stand there for a while, uncomfortable in each other's company.

I have to go actually.

DARREN. Raahhh. You just gonna leave me here?

MARK. What?

DARREN. I've just offered you company

MARK. Yeah / but...

DARREN. when you were wandering about like a twat

MARK. Thanks / but...

DARREN. on your own.

MARK. How come you're on your own?

,

,

Can I have a cigarette?

DARREN. Piss off.

,

MARK. / Right.

The school bell rings; they adjust their clothing.

Three

Cars passing.

DARREN. Right. Listen, yeah.

(As if someone in the audience is checking their phone.) Oi, listen.

Some bits of the story are just about me, yeah, coz I'm sick and Mark's a pussy.

So.

DARREN *is hanging around Brentford, suspended from school. Bored, lonely, wired.*

It's week two of Year 10 and Miss Flappy-Flaps has suspended me.

But, look, hey, all I'm saying is… world keeps spinning, cars keep rolling past… pointless really. And I feel like I feel like I'm floating… suspended.

He bounces back, big smile, covering the blip.

So. Do you know what I do? Do you? No. You don't. What I do, yeah, in times like these, is I go on little soirées into the world. I go McDonald's at the top of Brentford High Street fam and I walk through the Drive-Thru.

I *walk* through the *Drive*-Thru. And BEHOLD! An adventure of gigantic proportions…

He walks through the Drive-Thru.

Straight up, the woman is like – (*As McDonald's employee.*) 'Excuse me, we can't serve you unless you're in a vehicle.'

And I say I'm on the vehicle of my legs innit. The first ever vehicle that existed, yeah?

And she's like, 'Your legs are not a vehicle.'

And I'm like, why you looking at my legs for man, you a pervert?

And she's like, 'Can Josente please come to window two please. Josente to window two.'

And I'm like NO. I want twelve nuggets, bitch. With spicy mayo.

And I show it to her. Just for one second innit. Little flash, glint in the pocket.

I lock her eyes to mine.

She goes away.

I wait.

She comes back.
Hands me twelve nuggets in a box in a bag.
I look in the bag. No spicy mayo.
I look at her. Don't even have to say it.
She dashes to get the sauce, chucks it in, hands shaking.

I depart on my vehicle.

I start eating them by the canal. I drop one and a couple of pigeons reckon they're getting involved; I kick 'em away with my bless Reeboks, which are second hand but still bless.

I feel in my pocket and my blade is gone.

He checks all his pockets and (inexplicably) fully checks in his pants and socks.

Gone. I panic, thinking someone's gonna shank me with my own knife innit. And then I realise... never had it in the first place. Just imagined it. Got confused. And I feel fucking powerful coz the woman must of just give me the nuggets just coz she knows that I'm the fucking king.

I am. People know me round here innit.

MARK *appears and in their separate stories they nearly collide, but not quite.*

MARK. It's week two of Year 10 and I'm in RE. I like the RE classroom. It smells like wood varnish and incense.

DARREN. I get home, thinking I'll give the rest of the nuggets to Dad but he's like 'SUSPENDED? AGAIN? CHRIST DARREN... I've not got the time for this.'

I sit next to Ryan who is ginger and people call him Ginger.

(Getting upset, everything catching up with him.) And I'm just like trying to do a nice thing for him and he

just throws it all back in my face. And he's full of bullshit anyway coz he has got time. Got plenty of time. Does fuck-all all day. Just lies in bed with his butters girlfriend.

He's got a bad back. Used to be a builder. Fell off a building.

Didn't die though, did he? (*Laughs, not quite sure why.*)

Me and Ryan have had two conversations. One when he needed a pen and one when he thought that invaluable meant 'of no value' and I explained it meant the opposite.

'SUSPENDED? AGAIN? CHRIST DARREN... I've not got the energy.'

This is the most I've spoken to anyone and I wonder if Ryan might be a potential friend. But I find myself just, sort of...wary. Looking for...

Even though I'm still hungry, I throw the nuggets at my dad and dash for the door.

Ryan, I ask, do you know where Darren is?

DARREN *runs off.*

MARK. 'Got suspended innit,' Ryan says.

Do you know when he'll be back? I ask.

Ryan shrugs.

He doesn't care, why would he?

Then he asks me if I want to go common after school.

It takes me a while to register that he's inviting me out. To a thing. Outside school.

I think for a moment. Barney will be waiting for me by the door for his walk – Barney is my dog and he can tell the time.

But then I remember that I've got no actual friends and Barney is just a dog.

So I say yes.

Half-light and a chair scraping back, classroom to café.

Four

Now.

MARK. So the reason I'm telling you now, yeah. Is because he's here. In the café. Mum thinks I'm wasting myself in this job. Like I'm too smart for it or something. But work. It's like a ritual. Just a normal ritual that people have, that I'm part of. Keeps me... keeps me...

Three flat whites, two soya lattes, one spicy avo on rye. It's all students and MacBooks and low lights and they all think I'm depressed in an arty way but I'm actually depressed in a depressed way. (*Weird laugh.*) Better than I was before though.

Three English breakfast, two sticky flapjacks, one blueberry muffin.

The bell above the café door tinkles.

And now he's *here* standing *here* bold as brass, sticking out like a fucking dinosaur from my past, having the the fucking nerve, to exist. My colleague, Edu, looks at me like 'who's this' and

No one should ever have to do this. No one should ever have to.

MARK *is suctioned back into the story.*

Five

The common. Sounds of teenagers; shouting, music, screechy laughter.

DARREN. This is the common. Common ground. The land of the people.

MARK. Ryan invited me but has forgotten I'm here and is deep in the process of getting his tongue inside the minty mouths of the girls that straggle around, the 'hot' ones with legs like toothpicks. I sit amongst a pile of bags, staring at bloated cigarette butts tangled in the grass and scroll through photos of Barney on my phone, trying not to make eye contact with Darren, who is striding about with this girl attached to him on a short leash – a shared earphone.

But then suddenly he lets her off the leash and she's coming towards me. I focus crazily on photos of Barney in the garden.

That's Blaize. She's basically the hottest girl at the girls' school and we're like going out, or whatever. We have sex like all the time. Like every. fucking. day. It's madness. Blows the mind.

The girl is looking for something, she's going 'where is it... I swear I left it here?!' And I say, are you looking for something?

(*Noticing* MARK *talking to Blaize*.) The fuck is he doing here?

She's looking for her tobacco. Darren wants a cigarette.

I silently help her look for it.

'

Turns out I'm sitting on it and it's warm and flat now. I hand it to her and she says 'thanks' at the same time that I say sorry.

We have nothing else to say.

She looks down at my phone, sees the picture of Barney wearing his special Christmas waistcoat that I made. Instinctively, I lock the phone, embarrassed of the baubles.

'That your dog?' she says. 'Cute waistcoat.'

God bless you Barney.
Everyone loves a Labrador.
I show her more pictures.
Barney swimming, Barney
asleep on my bed. And we
get into a good chat
because she's got a dog too.
It's a pug called Muggle
and she's bought him a
waistcoat that lights up so
she can see him when they
go on walks in the dark.

But suddenly a flash of arms
and legs and elbows and I'm
pushed forward and my
hand makes contact with her
rock-solid bra padding and I
start to sweat profusely.

DARREN *runs at* MARK,
and takes his phone.

She says 'Oi!' And I sit up,
panicking, and I ask if
she's okay and then I
realise my phone's gone.

DARREN *climbs out of reach with* MARK*'s phone.*

DARREN. Eurgh that's butters man. Your dog sleeps in your
bed.

Bruv! Bruv, look.

Mark's banging a dog.

MARK. Give it back.

,

What's your problem?

DARREN. What's my problem? You saying there's a problem?

MARK. No. I just... can I have my phone?

DARREN *looks at* MARK *for a long time.*

Everyone is watching.

Beg for it.

,

,

MARK (*sotto*). No.

DARREN. Hands together.

MARK (*trying to laugh it off*). Come on.

DARREN. On your knees.

MARK. What?

DARREN. On your knees.

,

MARK. No. I'm not gonna do that.

DARREN. Fine.

   DARREN *puts the phone in his pocket.*

MARK. Wait!

DARREN (*leaving*). Blaize. Come.

Six

*Half-light and heavy breathing; the sound of someone running,
being chased. They move to new positions.*

MARK. The next day my form
tutor reads out the names of
people in detention and it's
me and Darren.

DARREN. Detention's
actually sick yeah coz you
get juice and biscuits. Coz
they can't keep you in
school that long without

And I was like why am I in detention? And she was like – (*Northern Irish*.) 'You know why.' And I was like, no I don't. And she was like 'Do you really want to discuss this in front of the whole class, Mark? I don't think you do,' which made it all doubly confusing and now I have to spend an hour in a room with a person who I reckon could probably –

MARK *tenses up a little, but tries to act like everything is normal, clears his throat.*

This is the first ever detention I've ever had in my life. It's weird. It's like… neither the teacher nor the students are supposed to be here. The teacher is in her office next door. It feels, kind of, secret. (*Whisper.*) Like no one knows we're here.

providing food innit. That's a fact.

DARREN *walks into detention.*

Alright Markie?

DARREN. Oi. I said ALRIGHT MARKIE. Are you dumb?

MARK. Yeah. Hi.

DARREN. What brings you to detention young man?

MARK. I don't actually know. You?

DARREN. Oh miss just keeps me here coz she fancies me innit. It's usually just me and her so we just, you know… bang on the desk.

MARK. You serious?

DARREN *bursts out laughing*.

DARREN. You're such a twat.

They fidget for a bit. DARREN *eventually sits down*.

Ain't you gonna ask for your phone back?

MARK (*aside*). I've planned for this. I'm just gonna pretend I don't want it. Don't care about it. Reverse psychology.

MARK (*shrugging, casual*). Nah. Don't need it.

DARREN. Good. Coz I don't have it no more anyway.

MARK *shrugs*.

Had to hand it in.

MARK *looks up*.

MARK. Why?

DARREN. I think you know why.

MARK. What you on about?

DARREN. I had no choice. Imagine if a Year 7 had saw it, man.

MARK. Saw what?

DARREN. Tight Slut Takes Rough Anal.

MARK. What?!

DARREN. Twenty-seven minutes of it. Bookmarked.

,

That's… that's not cool, man.

MARK. Have you… did you like, set me up?

DARREN *shrugs, 'maybe'*.

What the fuck? How did you even get into my phone?

DARREN *shrugs*.

DARREN. We've got the same birthday.

MARK. What?

DARREN. Could be twins.

MARK. Did you guess my passcode?

DARREN. Just saying. Tight Slut Takes Rough Anal.

MARK. Could you stop saying that.

DARREN. I thought you were cool, man.

MARK. Well, I am.

DARREN. So you're admitting to it?

MARK. No! I'm not admitting to it! You… you set me up! I could get excluded!

DARREN. Okay. Jesus. Calm yourself. Have some juice.

DARREN passes MARK a juice box.

You're quite jokes when you're stressed.

MARK looks at the juice. Angrily, he pokes the straw through the hole and drinks. DARREN drinks his own juice, with his eyes on MARK the whole time.

The slurping of the juice gets louder and could be mistaken for choking.

Seven

Now.

MARK. In the café. Darren's standing a little distance away from the till, watching me.

And this customer has sort of stepped around him to order and she's ordering. She's definitely saying words but I've lost all my basic skills. Like moving and speaking and listening and responding.

It's been four years. And now he's –

(*To customer.*) Four years. I mean four pounds. One
GreenPower Juice. Four pounds.

Contactless beep.

(*Clears throat.*) Would you like your receipt?

The sound of the receipt printing, then MARK *is suctioned
back into the story.*

Eight

MARK. Darren hasn't been at school for a few days and there's
been these lads from Year 11… just sort of watching me do
stuff. I go to the fountain to fill up my water and they're just
watching. I go to the library to get a book and when I come
out, they're outside. When I leave school, they follow me all
the way to the top of my road.

They don't do anything. They're just. There. And…

It's afternoon registration in our form group. People wander
in but no one sits next to me and I pretend it doesn't bother
me. I pretend I haven't spent the whole day alone.

Darren turns up. Late.

DARREN *enters.*

DARREN. Safe, miss.

MARK. My mum found out about the whole phone-hacking
thing and I'm fairly sure he got suspended for it and I'm
fairly sure now that he's back he'll probably kill me. Or pay
those lads to kill me. In fact, maybe he already has. Maybe
that's why they – The only seat left is the one next to me. He
takes the seat and my chest hurts when he looks at me. His
anger floating near me like ripples around a shark. I can feel
it like it's my own feelings.

My mum does say I'm a sponge, like when they were
divorcing I could feel it happen before it actually happened.

DARREN *slumps on the desk.*

This is the closest I've ever been to him. I glance down and I see that his shirt is dirty at the cuffs and his nails are dirty and there are scratches and cuts on his arms and I suddenly feel this pang of…

Like maybe he needs help and maybe nobody loves him and nobody ever will. And I say

Darren, I'm really sorry. It's just, my mum was asking all these questions about, like, cyberbullying, and… I didn't mean to get you suspended.

DARREN *sits up. A strange and tangled pause.*

DARREN. Didn't get suspended.

MARK. What?

DARREN. Holiday innit.

,

MARK. Oh. I thought you got suspended.

DARREN. Nope. Holiday.

,

MARK. Cool. Where did you go?

DARREN. Barbados.

MARK. For three days?

DARREN. You been counting the days?

MARK (*quickly*). No.

So umm how was it then? Barbados.

DARREN. Hot.

Turtles.

Beaches with like… umbrellas.

Sombreros.

MARK. Sombreros? In Barbados?

DARREN. Yeah.

And sharks.

MARK. Sharks?

A blip; a shifty sense that DARREN *has heard* MARK*'s thoughts.*

DARREN. Loads of sharks.

Bare fit girls.

,

And I had sex with like... all of them.

MARK. You had sex with all the girls in Barbados?

DARREN (*giving* MARK *a look like knives*). Don't believe me?

MARK. What about Blaize?

DARREN. I can show you my dick innit. It's got burns.

MARK. No... just...um... you know... send me a postcard next time.

DARREN *looks up. People don't usually ask him for stuff. He is almost angry, but then laughs it off.*

DARREN. You're weird man.

MARK. Sorry.

DARREN. You still a loner?

MARK. No. I just... I'm just... it takes me a long time to –

DARREN. Bruv chill I'm joking man.

MARK. Oh.

,

Hey, you know those lads in the year above?

DARREN. What, Tariq and that?

MARK. Yeah. Are they your mates?

DARREN (*shrugs*). They're from my estate.

MARK. They've been kind of like… do you, like, hang out
  with them?

DARREN. You been spyin on me?

MARK. No.

DARREN. Knew you were a pervert.

MARK. What?

DARREN. That's why I liked you innit.

  MARK *is confused. So is* DARREN. *Neither of them was
  expecting to admit they enjoy each other's company.*

  The school bell rings.

  You going canteen?

MARK. Yeah. You?

DARREN. Got no P.

MARK (*shrugs*). I'll get you / something.

DARREN. Piss off.

MARK. I was just offering.

DARREN. Don't need offers.

  MARK *goes to leave.*

  Oi. Mark. Wait.

  MARK *stops.*

  I'll come with you. See if they have any bacon rolls left.

  MARK *smiles. Lights flicker, the sound of bacon frying…*

Nine

…becomes the sound of a shower running.

MARK *is standing in his room, holding a baggy of weed aloft like a trophy.*

MARK. Look. See? That right there. That is evidence of friendship.

DARREN *is in the shower.*

DARREN. So basically yeah, you know on the common. When I said me and Blaize have sex like every day. (*A real threat to someone in the audience.*) Don't fucking tell anyone yeah, but that was a lie innit.

Darren gave this to me. I bought him some lunch and then after school he… just gave me this like 'you want this?'

(*Drying off, getting dressed.*) We're having sex tonight though. First time.

Not like my first time. Not like first time ever in my life. I just mean first time with her. Obviously.

(*If someone laughs:*) Dickhead.

And I've bought Rizla, tobacco, a grinder and a lighter. So now I just have to figure out how to… roll it. And then I can be like. Hey Darren come meet me on the common… or something.

The doorbell rings. DARREN *jumps up and down excitedly.*

(*Opens his laptop and types into YouTube.*) 'How to Roll a Joint.'

'Put your weed into your grinder and twist it clockwise and counter-clockwise.'

'Now make your roach. Use the card off the rolling paper.'

MARK *copies the guy in the video.*

'Spread your weed evenly along the paper.'

MARK *continues following the instructions until he has a wonky finished product.*

Shit man... COMING!

He runs off to get the door.

DARREN *is swinging around in excitement.*

I open the door and she's right there, looking fly, and I'm like

Hi Blaize.

And she's like, 'Your dad's definitely out for the whole night, yeah?' And I'm like yeah definitely. And I take her hand and pull her close to me and close the door.

And she's like, 'We definitely doin this, yeah?' And she's got this hungry look. And it's just her an' me now. And instead of feeling... like... horny... I get this feeling like maybe I'm gonna shit myself?

And I'm just like wondering... Is this normal?

She starts kissing me and she takes my hand and puts it between her legs. And I'm kind of like whoa. I thought I was gonna be

Ta-dah!

He opens the window and lights the joint.

The room fills with smoke.

Fuuuuuck me.

(*Whisper to audience.*) It's okay. My mum's at Zumba.

I feel soft like all the corners of my mind are smudged. And I see us laughing and laughing behind the AstroTurf at lunch and I try to think of a present to give him back. Something really really good.

---

making the moves innit. And she whispers that she's really excited and she's wanted to do this for a really long time and my mind just goes blank like there's this fog.

The room fills with smoke.

She's got her soft hand down my trousers but it's like I can't feel anything at all.

My dick is hard but there's this fog, and I try to focus but it goes soft.

And Blaize is like 'What's wrong?' And I'm like can we just... can you just kiss me again and she does and it feels all soft and wet and I want to get away so I push her and then she's down on the floor but I didn't mean to.

She's crying and shouting and I say that I'm sorry... I don't know what happened... and she shouts and I shout back coz I've already said I'm sorry, and she leaves.

I pick up my phone to message him but I realise I haven't actually got his number.

He continues smoking his joint.

The door slams. DARREN kneels on the floor with his forehead on the carpet, making angry noises.

After a while he sits up. Finds his box, gets out a joint and lights it, adding to the fog in the room. He stumbles a bit, sits down.

Do you ever get confused about like, memories?

Feel like I'm falling over.

I feel like I might fall and keep on falling forever. And he would catch me.

He inhales wrong and starts to cough.

He inhales wrong and starts to cough.

Maybe they catch each other, almost dreamlike: MARK *is imagining it.*

DARREN. Alright, Markie?

Ten

Now.

MARK, *still coughing, waves at the air to clear the smoke, clear his mind.*

MARK. In the café. She takes her receipt and goes away, juicy, contactless.

And he's here.

MARK *and* DARREN. Alright Markie?

MARK. No one should have to do this... he's really looking at me, like he's left something inside me and he's trying to find it.

And I see that he's quite pale, probably from spending four years inside, and the scars on his arms are faded. If you didn't know exactly where they were, you wouldn't know they were there.

I realise I haven't moved or responded and I say to the till, as if it's alive and listening,

Alright Darren? Didn't know you were out.

DARREN. Really? Thought you'd be counting the days.

MARK. No.

Should I tell him? If he knew all the things I'd thought about him for the past four years, I don't think he'd be here right now, because sometimes I'd get a knife and reopen the wound and I'd sit in the bath, in my own blood,

because sometimes, I just wanted to feel something.

DARREN. Yeah I'm out now. Free to roam.

MARK. And I swing right back.

MARK *swings back into the story.*

Eleven

School. Geography.

DARREN *is distracted.* MARK *is focused.*

DARREN (*to teacher*). What, miss?

,

(*To teacher.*) Miss, man. I *was* listening.

,

Dunno miss… is it rain?

MARK (*quietly*). Percolation. Percolation followed by groundwater discharge.

DARREN. Urgh.

MARK. What?

DARREN. Discharge.

MARK. Groundwater discharge. / That's basically how rivers exist.

DARREN. Miss man – (*Shooting his hand up in the air.*) Mark is being dirty.

MARK *tries to prevent* DARREN *putting his hand up.*

DARREN *shrieks.*

Aah! Don't touch me with your discharge hands man.

MARK. Darren!

DARREN. You're so fucking dirty.

MARK *writes something down off the board, trying to ignore* DARREN, *who swings on his chair.*

Did you know I've got two mice? They're called Mac and Cheese.

MARK *focuses on his work, ignoring* DARREN.

Found 'em under a hedge. Took 'em home in a Big Mac box.

MARK *focuses on his work, ignoring* DARREN.

Used to have three but they attacked the small one coz it was a little runt like you.

MARK *continues to focus on his work.*

Sometimes I put them up my bum.

MARK *stops writing, and looks up.*

DARREN *stops swinging, cracking up.*

Your face man! You're such a twat.

,

(*To teacher.*) Sorry miss. Mark is bare distracting me, innit.

MARK. Darren...

DARREN. Yes bruv.

MARK. You're actually really distracting me. This could come up in the mock exam.

DARREN. FAM. Have a bit of gratefulness innit.

MARK. Why?

DARREN. I saved your life innit.

MARK. You did not save my life.

DARREN. How come you're alive then?

,

MARK. I don't need you to like... protect me.

DARREN. Bruv.

MARK. What? I don't.

DARREN. Yes you do.

MARK. It's embarrassing.

DARREN. Embarrassing?

MARK. Yeah.

DARREN. You sayin you're embarrassed by me?

MARK. Nah. I'm saying you don't need to protect me.

DARREN. Those lads are taking the piss mate. Are you just gonna take that?

MARK. You're making it worse.

DARREN. Mark man. You're scared to go to the toilet. In case they come in. Innit.

,

Just admit it. You don't take a shit till you go home.

Coz you're shook.

,

Exactly. So.

You do need me. Otherwise, eventually...

,

you'll just shit yourself.

MARK. Shut up Darren.

DARREN (*shocked by* MARK*'s change of tone*). What?

MARK. Stop being a prick.

DARREN (*anger rising*). BRUV.

MARK. You need *me*.

DARREN. No I don't.

MARK. Who buys your lunch every day?

DARREN. What you saying?

MARK. What would you eat if I wasn't in?

DARREN. Don't need to eat at school. Eat like a king when I get home innit.

They both know this isn't true.

You better watch what you say, Mark.

MARK *over-focuses on his work.* DARREN *angrily opens his book and starts writing stuff down off the board.*

MARK (*sotto*). Sorry.

DARREN. What?

MARK. I said sorry. I didn't mean –

The bell goes. DARREN *gets up, leaves, knocking* MARK*'s workbook off the table.*

Twelve

The school bell becomes the tinkly bell above the café door – a more intense and uncomfortable bell than before.

MARK. In the café. I want to run away and hold on to him and punch him in the face, all at once.

DARREN. I been going on walks, roaming about, and I saw you innit. Here. In your apron. And then I saw you again. And then I thought. I should come say hi. (*Big weird smile.*)

Though we could catch up.

MARK. Catch up?

(*Aside.*) Catch. Up, he says, as if we're just two regular people... Okay Darren, let's catch up. Let's catch up about the time I very very nearly jumped under a train. Let's catch up about the time I opened the car door on the motorway and I wanted the rush of the tarmac to rip me up. Let's catch up about the cutting and the burning and the relief and the blood, and the choking on all of it. Let's catch up about that.

DARREN (*directing this to the till*). Coz you know, before juvie and that, you were like my best mate, innit.

MARK finally looks at DARREN properly, unable to believe that he has admitted this, and despite everything, he laughs.

MARK. You were my only mate.

They spin back into the story.

Thirteen

They pace in opposite directions.

MARK*'s doorbell.*

MARK. I get home from school.

DARREN*'s doorbell.*

DARREN. I get home from school.

Got no key coz Dad's butters girlfriend has it, so I stick my hand through the letterbox and do my nifty trick with the latch.

Barney's waiting by the door and when I come in he puts his furry head against my leg. He wants some love and I give him loads of love and he loves it. (*Talking to Barney.*) Don't you Barney?

Dad's asleep on the sofa, roll of fat falling out the bottom of his T-shirt. His drugs are on the table. I could take some but I don't. Too risky.

Mum opens with her usual thrilling conversation starter: 'How was school, pickle?'

I tiptoe past him to my room and close the door. It's freezing. I put on my Nike jumper over the top of my school jumper. And I'm still cold. I get into my bed, under the cover.

And I know she's thinking, did those boys follow you home again? Have you

made any friends yet?
Being friends with Darren
is like being friends with a
tornado. Most of the time
he's just destroying stuff,
but there's this calm bit in
the middle that you catch if
you're standing in just the
right...

'Darren!?' Dad shouts from
the living room. I really
don't wanna deal with him
right now. I don't wanna
see his sagging face and his
sagging skin and I prop my
chair up against the door. I
don't let him in because I
know what he wants me to
do and I'm not doing it.

School was alright, I say to
Mum. I've made a friend.
Kind of.

'Darren! DARREN!' Bang
bang bang – he's wrestlin'
with the door, tryin' to get
in. He wants me to sell for
him but but – (*More
banging*.) ahhhh he can sell
his own fucking drugs!

Mum's trying to hide how
pleased she is about my one
friend. 'That's great,
Markie,' she says, 'That's
really, great! Why don't you
invite him round?!' she says.

And I stay wrapped in my
duvet, muffling the sound
of him, wishing I had
somewhere else to go. But
I don't.

I'm not going to invite him
round Mum, I say. People
don't do that.

DARREN *circles the stage.*

MARK *circles the stage in
the opposite direction.*

Fourteen

MARK *and* DARREN *arrive in the same place: outside*
MARK*'s house.*

MARK (*aside*). I don't quite know how it happened but Darren's
    come round my house tonight. My mum's making a quiche.

DARREN. That your house?

MARK. Yeah.

DARREN. That your front door?

MARK. Yeah.

DARREN. This is weird, man.

> ,

Is your mum in?

MARK. Dunno. Why?

DARREN. Saw her in the school office. She's well hot.

MARK. Darren!?

DARREN. What?

MARK. Don't.

DARREN. Bruv chill, was just wondering if she's in.

> ,

What we gonna do?

MARK. Dunno... hang out.

DARREN. Where?

MARK. In my room?

DARREN. On your bed?

MARK. No. What?

DARREN. This is weird man.

DARREN *stares at the front door, suspicious.*

MARK. I've got some of that weed left.

,

And I've got a TV in my room.

DARREN. Is it?

MARK. Yeah.

,

DARREN. Fine.

DARREN *heads towards the door.* MARK *opens it.*

Barney barks, excitedly. The noise fills the space, unpleasant and shrill. DARREN *leaps away from the door.*

AH. Fucking hell. You didn't say you had a dog, bruv.

MARK *strokes Barney, ad libbing, dog talk.* DARREN *doesn't move.*

MARK. Hello Barney! He's just excited, aren't you, Barney?

Come on, it's fine.

DARREN *isn't convinced.*

Don't you like dogs?

DARREN. They bite.

MARK. Barney doesn't bite. Out of the two of you, I'd say you're more likely to bite. Look at him.

More dog talk: 'You don't bite do you Barney...', etc.

DARREN *is scared of Barney, but is trying to hide it.* MARK *realises.*

You okay?

DARREN. Yeah. (*No.*)

MARK (*to Barney*). Barney. Go to your bed. To your bed.

Barney trots away, the barking stops.

He'll calm down now –

DARREN. I think I'll just head home actually bruv.

MARK. Oh. Okay. Sorry I / should of

DARREN. See ya

DARREN *leaves.*

MARK *stands still for a long time.*

MARK (*deadly serious in a very teenage way*). I have never been angry at Barney before. This is the first time. He ruined it. It's ruined now.

He throws his backpack down.

DARREN. I get home and go straight to my room. I give some food to my mice. The sound of the dog is ringing in my ears so I put my speaker on as loud as it goes.

MARK *shouts the following over the music, we hardly hear him:*

MY MUM GETS HOME FROM SAINSBURY'S. 'WHERE'S YOUR FRIEND?' SHE ASKS.

WHAT? I SAY, DISTRACTED. I FEEL LIKE I CAN'T MOVE, CAN'T HEAR MYSELF THINK. I'M JUST STANDING HERE IN

DARREN*'s music plays deafeningly loud. He starts to dance to calm himself down.*

THE CORRIDOR LIKE
AN IDIOT.

'WHERE'S YOUR
FRIEND?' SHE SAYS
AGAIN. 'I'VE BOUGHT
STUFF FOR DINNER.'

DUNNO, I SAY.

'WASN'T HE SUPPOSED
TO BE COMING ROUND
TODAY?' SHE ASKS.

NAH, I SAY. NAH. YOU
MUST'VE GOT YOUR
DAYS MUDDLED UP
MUM.

'SO WHEN'S HE
COMING THEN?' SHE
ASKS.

DUNNO, I SAY.

I turn around and go to my
room, a lump growing in
my throat. It's ruined now.

MY DAD SLAMS INTO
MY ROOM AND TURNS
OFF MY MUSIC.

The music stops. DARREN
*stops dancing; he breathes
heavily.*

He's pissed off because
he's been in the next room,
trying to fuck his butters
girlfriend and I've come in
and played my music and

(*Suddenly, as his dad.*)
'What the fuck do you
think this is Darren, a
fucking nightclub?'

He pushes me against the
wall, holding me there with

all his weight on me and I can't move. 'Either get out of my house,' he says 'or keep the fucking noise down.'

Fine I say. I'll fuck off then, shall I? Out of your way. So you can have sex with that fat woman and leave me the fuck alone.

Barney is on *my* bed even though I told him to go to *his* bed and he knows the difference.

I push him off the bed and say GET DOWN and it's the closest I've ever come to hitting him but he looks confused and sad and I slide off the bed and cry into his furry head.

I push him off me / and head out into the night.

DARREN *circles the stage.*

DARREN *stops by* MARK*'s front door.*

The doorbell rings. Barney starts barking. MARK *looks up, confused, wiping his eyes.*

It rings again.

He opens the door.

DARREN. Can I come in?

,

MARK. What about Barney?

DARREN. Can you put him in the garden?

MARK *stares at* DARREN, *with a million questions, but says nothing. He disappears to put Barney in the garden (we hear dog-talk from offstage).* DARREN *stands awkwardly on the doorstep. Maybe he does something weird.*

MARK *returns. He checks his watch.*

MARK. It's like, ten-thirty.

DARREN. So?

MARK. So are you, like, staying over?

DARREN. Just lemme in man.

DARREN *comes in, suddenly standing very close to* MARK *in the narrow hallway.*

MARK *smiles for the first time in ages.*

MARK. You hungry?

Fifteen

Now.

Café sounds – the bell tinkles, harsher again.

MARK. You were my only mate.

DARREN. How come you never came to visit me?

MARK (*aside*). And suddenly I'm back there and I can see him bleeding and burning for me and I want to reach out to him but I can't.

DARREN. Not one single person visited me apart from a lawyer.

MARK. A lawyer? / What for?

DARREN. Not even on my birthday. Our birthday.

MARK (*sotto, looking around the café*). Darren – as if I was going to visit you in prison. You're not even supposed to be in contact with me.

DARREN. Alright, didn't realise you were the fucking thought police.

MARK. I mean the actual *police* police?

,

DARREN. Don't be such a bellend man, I'm not on a tag.

MARK. Oh good, great! So you can just do whatever you want then. Take a seat, have a muffin, let's catch up.

DARREN (*sotto*). Just wanted to see you.

They slide back into the story.

Sixteen

DARREN *enters, bouncing a ball, wearing a sports bib, deep in thought.*

MARK *enters, also in a sports bib, and stands a sheepish distance away from* DARREN. *There is a morning-after feeling.*

MARK. Alright.

DARREN *is slightly startled by* MARK*'s presence and miss-bounces the ball. It rolls away and he doesn't reach to get it.*

DARREN. Safe.

They both think of things to say but don't say them.

MARK. You... umm...

DARREN *shrugs.*

DARREN. Do you want to go somewhere?

MARK. What, now?

DARREN. Yeah. Let's go.

DARREN *is taking off his sports bib.*

Do you have a bike?

MARK. Yeah but it's at home.

DARREN. Bet it's like pink with tassels on it that Mummy bought you innit.

MARK. Nah I've actually got a really good bike.

DARREN. *Nah I've actually got a really good bike.*

MARK. You don't even have a bike.

DARREN. I can get one.

MARK. We'll miss benchball.

DARREN. Bruv.

MARK. What?

DARREN. No one wants you on their team anyway.

    DARREN *exits*.

MARK (*shouting after him*). How would you know? You never even come to PE.

    After a moment, the ball comes flying at MARK *from the wings. He does not catch it.*

    (*Sotto.*) Whatever.

    He takes off his sports bib and follows DARREN. *They arrive at the school bike shed.*

DARREN. Ta-dah!

MARK. What?

DARREN. Bikes.

MARK. These are other people's bikes.

DARREN (*mock*). Oh are they, I didn't realise.

MARK. They're locked.

    DARREN *opens his backpack to reveal a large pair of wire cutters*.

    Jesus – where'd you get them?

DARREN. Caretaker's cupboard innit. There's bare shit in there. Saws, hammers, axes.

MARK. Axes? Why does the caretaker have axes?

DARREN. To shank you and feed you to the pigeons innit.

> DARREN *looks over his shoulder. Coast is clear. He goes towards one of the bikes with the cutters.*

MARK. Wait wait, what you doing? Are you... are we... what you doing?

DARREN. Fucking hell Mark. Stop waving your lanky arms and go and keep watch.

MARK. Keep watch? It's broad daylight.

DARREN. Look yeah. Do you want to come, or not?

MARK. I dunno.

DARREN. What else you gonna do?

> MARK *considers this.*

MARK. Fine.

> *He puts out his hand to take the cutters.*

DARREN. Really?

MARK. Yeah.

> MARK *cuts the cable lock.*

Seventeen

Richmond Park. DARREN *is giving* MARK *a backie on the stolen bike. Angry beeping keels past dangerously.*

DARREN. Bruv you do not need to hold on to me / that tight.

MARK. I have nothing else to hold on to!

DARREN. Just... balance.

They lose balance and topple over in a heap. They swear under their breath, they are both quite hurt but they laugh hysterically until they can hardly breathe.

,

,

Fuuuucking hell.

MARK. Darren, have you ever ridden a bike before?

DARREN. That was your fault. You're too lanky, man.

MARK. We nearly got hit by a bus.

DARREN *shrugs.*

DARREN. Bus drivers are cunts.

MARK. We were on the wrong side of the road.

DARREN. Shut up man, you sound like my mum.

MARK *looks at* DARREN, *considering something.*

What?

MARK. Dunno, you've just never mentioned your mum before.

DARREN (*suddenly not laughing any more*). Yes I have.

MARK. Oh. Okay.

DARREN *covers the blip.*

DARREN. This park is siiick. It's like proper wilderness innit.

,

MARK *looks around.*

MARK. Yeah.

DARREN *slumps down in the long grass, relaxing in the sun.* MARK *lays down next to him. After a while,* DARREN *opens his eyes. He sees a large creature in the distance.*

DARREN. The fuck is that?

MARK *looks.*

MARK. It's a deer.

DARREN. Sick horns. (*To deer.*) Oi, RUDOLF.

MARK. Shhh. You'll scare it.

The deer is walking. In silence, they follow it with their eyes. It's the first comfortable silence they've ever had.

The deer goes out of sight.

DARREN. Where's it going?

MARK. Dunno. Stag do?

MARK *is impressed with himself for making a joke. He looks to* DARREN *for affirmation but it's gone over his head.*

DARREN. What?

MARK. Doesn't matter.

They sit in silence for a bit more, looking out at the park.

How's things with Blaize?

DARREN. Blaize? Dumped her innit.

MARK. How come?

DARREN. Coz. She was like… bare frigid.

MARK. Thought you had sex like, every day?

DARREN. Why you wanna know my business for?

MARK. Just asking.

DARREN *turns to look at* MARK.

DARREN. Just askin'?

MARK. Yeah.

'

What?

DARREN. Nuffink.

DARREN *looks away.*

DARREN *looks at* MARK. MARK *looks up*. DARREN
quickly looks away.

MARK. Darren.

DARREN. What?

   ,

What?!

MARK. You're being…

DARREN. I'm being what?

MARK. Weird.

   ,

Is there…

MARK *looks around, slightly panicked, suddenly wary that
this whole trip could be a trap.*

Is anyone else coming? Is there something going on?

DARREN. You tell me, innit.

MARK. What?

DARREN. Is there? Somefink going on?

MARK. I don't know.

DARREN. I seen you, Mark.

   ,

I seen you looking at me.

MARK. What?

DARREN. I seen you looking at me. Like that.

MARK. Like what?

DARREN. You gonna deny it?

   ,

Go on. I swear down Mark – deny it.

,

,

MARK *stares at the ground, to prevent* DARREN *from reading his mind.*

MARK. I've seen you too.

DARREN. What?

MARK. I've seen you too. Looking at me.

DARREN. Bruv. You can fuck right off.

MARK. Well why did we come here then?

DARREN. I don't know, Mark. You're the bent one.

MARK *gets up, puts his bag on.*

MARK. You're full of shit.

He is about to leave –

DARREN. Where you goin'?

MARK. Home.

DARREN. Wait.

MARK. Why? (*Harsh.*) You wanna come round again?

DARREN. No.

,

MARK. Well what do you want, then?

MARK *goes to leave again.* DARREN *stops him.*

DARREN. I swear down Mark, why you denying it?

MARK. I'm not! You are.

DARREN *realises what* MARK *is saying.*

He takes MARK'*s hand. They stay like that for a moment.*

He lifts MARK'*s hand to his cheek. They stay like that for a moment.*

MARK *leans in and brushes his lips against* DARREN*'s other cheek.*

DARREN *pulls away.*

DARREN. Don't.

MARK. Okay. Sorry, I…

DARREN. I was just experimenting innit.

MARK. What?

DARREN. So don't fucking touch me.

MARK. But you just asked me to –

DARREN. You don't know me.

,

,

MARK. Yes I do. I do know you.

MARK *leans in again.* DARREN *jerks away and pins* MARK *to the ground.*

DARREN. Are you deaf? I said don't touch me.

MARK. Get off!

MARK *is angry and confused and he shoves* DARREN *with surprising force and they fight. They really fight – each hurting the other badly.*

DARREN *gets on top and pulls a knife.*

MARK *freezes. Neither of them move.*

DARREN. You think you can fight me you fag?

He pulls up MARK*'s school shirt and touches the blade against his stomach.* MARK *tries not to breathe.*

They hover like that for a moment.

I'll do it.

I'll fucking do it.

MARK. Do it then.

DARREN *doesn't move*.

DO IT.

DARREN *doesn't move*.

Knew you were a pussy.

DARREN *presses the blade down and* MARK *cries out in pain*.

DARREN *lets up*. MARK *staggers to his feet, clutching his stomach. He looks at* DARREN, *then dashes away*.

DARREN *stands there with the knife, breathing heavily. Maybe he considers hurting himself. His heavy breathing gets louder, surrounding him and becoming the sound of the wind in the long grass*.

Eighteen

The sound of the wind becomes the sound of the milk-frothing machine. Bell tinkles, now reaching a harsh and unpleasant tone.

MARK. In the café. My palms are sweating, my whole body has heated up because there's the bike and the deer and the knife and he's admitted I was his best mate. He's admitted that he wanted to see me. The thoughts spin around my mind stupidly as I zip through every moment, every look, every laugh… laughing to the point where it hurts and you can't breathe and you feel sick even, but you're still laughing.

And I realise that this heat, this hot feeling is joy. (*Happy/sad tears*.) And I realise how much I've missed it. My heart feels bigger. My face feels bigger because I'm smiling. He wants to see me. He wants to catch up. He wants me to be his best mate. It's all I've been wanting to hear but I didn't know I wanted to hear it.

I push all the other stuff away, because it doesn't matter. It never really mattered.

MARK *laughs a bit, at recognising a lost and dusty feeling of joy.*

DARREN. How are Mac and Cheese?

MARK (*aside*). He left them on my doorstep before he got locked up.

They... they had a good life.

DARREN. They dead?

MARK. I did look after them, I bought them this sick cage with like tubes and like three different levels, but mice don't really live that long, you know.

DARREN. Yeah. Nah. Fair enough.

MARK. D'you know what I was thinking. Wanted to ask you. What was the third one called?

DARREN. Eh?

MARK. You said, when we were in Geography, you said you had three mice but one was a runt and it died.

DARREN. Oh right. Salad.

MARK. Salad? You had a mouse called Salad?

DARREN. Yeah. Stupid, really.

They laugh, it gets warmer, and they enjoy the moment.

MARK. So, are you living back with your dad, in Brentford?

DARREN *is shifty, shakes his head.*

DARREN. Nah. He died last year.

MARK. What?! Darren. I'm... I'm so sorry. Shit. Did he...

DARREN. Yeah it was shit.

MARK. Did you... were you allowed out... to go to the... (funeral)?

DARREN (*shaking his head*). There wasn't really a funeral.

Neither of them speak for quite a long time. MARK *silently calculates that* DARREN *is now completely alone.*

Turns out the old man had some money though.

MARK. Really?

DARREN. Yeah, not much but like, I can keep the flat. That's why the lawyer...

MARK. Oh right, right.

DARREN. I've like... got money now. Feels weird.

,

MARK. You should go Barbados.

DARREN. Already been.

They laugh.

Nah. I'm doing a course. Business and Sport Science.

,

Gonna be a personal trainer.

MARK. You serious?

DARREN. Paid my course fees last night.

MARK. Wow, Darren, that's that's... amazing.

DARREN. Yeah. When I was a minor I was in this Offending Behaviour Programme, where you identify your strengths and your skills and shit... that's what I decided to do.

MARK (*aside*). I want to be happy for him. He's come out of prison, he's completely alone, and he's managed to... he's managed to actually do something. I can see that he's telling me because he's proud. I can see that he wants to show me –

DARREN. It's mad, isn't it. Like a fresh start.

MARK. It's great.

DARREN. Bet you're going uni and all? Bet you're going to one of the big ones innit.

MARK. No I. Nah.

DARREN. How come?

MARK *thinks for a moment about how much he can explain.*

MARK (*aside*). Because I dropped out? Because I had a breakdown? Because I tried to...

(*To* DARREN.) Because I don't have any... never got any A levels.

DARREN. Oh. Really? But you were like, bare smart.

They climb back into their story.

Nineteen

In the half-light, music blasts, cocktailed with distant police sirens. They run all over the playground, swinging, climbing, spinning.

MARK. It's nearly dark by the time I get home. Black-red blood has soaked through my shirt and I tie my jumper around my waist to cover it. I unlock the door with my hand shaking and go straight to my room / and lie down on the floor.

DARREN. I lie down in the grass for a long time. I lie there until it's completely dark and my clothes are wet and / I'm cold.

I'm cold and Barney starts licking me and I finally start to feel the pain. Sharp and sick. / Every time I try to move.

Every time I try to move, my body is like lead. I try to think. I don't have a key. I can't go home. I check my phone. No missed calls.

I could probably die out here and no one would care. I look at the knife again, / stomach seizing up like bricks.

Heaving these sobs which hurt my stomach and I try to hold them in but I can't and I don't really remember properly, like maybe I pass out for a bit…

Lights flicker.

Lights flicker.

…but my mum comes home and I lock myself in the bathroom and run the bath so she can't hear me crying with blood leaving my body in little / thin lines.

Thin lines mark the sky where planes have been and there's not one single star. I get on the bike and I cycle / in a straight line until I don't know where…

It's a straight thin line near my belly button. I clean it and wrap microporous tape around it and I take two of my mum's / sleeping pills.

I try to sleep in a tunnel in a playground but I'm shook coz there's noises and / I keep waking up.

I wake up to my mum asking me why I haven't got up for school. I tell her I'm ill and she says that I do / look a little 'peaky'.

I look outside the tunnel to check there's no kids about; it's empty and I slide out of the tunnel and I figure out that I'm in fucking Hanwell. I cycle back to Brentford, I get home, and I wait. / I sit by the door like a dog. (*He sits*

I sit somewhere bad outside myself, watching a

version of me trying to
figure out what just
happened, and some time
later, / my mum comes in
with some food.

*in a ball with his head in
his hands*.)

My dad comes home. And
he sees that my clothes are
wet and he sees that I'm
shivering and he sees that I
haven't slept and he sees the
blood and dirt on my hands.

And he doesn't say
anything. He just stares at
me like he doesn't know
me.

Then he opens the door and
goes in and he tells me to
get inside.

I go in and he

He asks me if I'm okay.

DARREN *shakes his head,
no*.

Why didn't you call me,
Dad? I've been... I've
been... I been out all night,
I say. Did you not care?

And I can see in his face,
for one little second,
something like guilt. A
realisation that he's my
only parent.

He looks at me and then he
goes away and I think fuck
you I knew you never gave
a shit, but then he comes
back with my duvet and my
trackies and he helps me
take my wet clothes off and
put the warm dry clothes on

and he wraps me in my duvet on the sofa and I cling on to him because the last time he hugged me was when / Mum died.

Mum definitely knows there's something wrong coz normally I'd be more worried about missing school. And she says, 'Have you and Darren had a falling out, love?'

A falling out. A falling out?! He fucking stabbed me, Mum.

But I don't say that. I can't tell her. I can't tell anyone because... I can't / lose him.

Later he brings me a hot chocolate and I must have fallen asleep on the sofa.

Lights flicker.

Lights flicker.

Coz when I wake up he's...

...washed all my clothes and he's ordered pizza. Madness. This same man who hits me and steals my weed. I realise I haven't eaten since yesterday morning. We just eat in silence for a bit and watch TV. It's nice.

And then he turns to me and he says that I don't have to tell him what happened, but if there's anything I want to talk about, / I can talk to him.

I want to talk to him. I pick up my phone, but you

can't just call the person
who stabbed you. Can
you? I try wearing the
feeling of being angry at
Darren but it doesn't fit.
Doesn't stick.

'I know sometimes I'm…
not around,' he says,
'but… you can talk to me. /
I'm your dad.'

Mum goes out to work
again and I get up and I
change my bandage and it
hurts slightly less, which
means he's further away
and I lie there feeling more
empty than I've ever felt
like I've shat out all my
organs and lost all my
blood and all that's left is
my brain but it doesn't
have anything to connect
to and I realise that my
only feeling is… I'm
desperate to… because we
were about to… you
know…

I open my laptop.

Chrome. Incognito.
PornHub.

I know exactly what I want
and I find it and I start
touching myself and it
feels amazing. My body
doesn't feel like mine, coz
of the painkillers and the
sleeping pills and
somehow that makes it all
better; makes it feel like
someone else is doing it.

I get very close to coming but the microporous tape unsticks and the cut reopens and blood starts trickling out and it fucking stings.

I pause it and / press escape.

Coz maybe it'll be an escape, telling Dad. My thoughts are all frozen / and I could let them out.

But the whole thing freezes. A pop-up appears with a red exclamation mark 'Your computer has a virus. You may lose some or all of your files. / Back up now.'

I back up. Right to the beginning. I tell him everything. I tell him about Mark, I tell him about the things that I want to do. I tell him everything. I give him everything. Every little thing. And I'm shook to say it all out loud. I'm / sweating.

Palms sweating, I panic. Force quit, shut down, escape, escape. It's completely frozen on a very revealing / still.

Still still still giving him everything, and he's not even looking at me and I've got nothing / left.

Nothing works and my mum's coming up the stairs, saying she's made chicken soup.

And I say, don't come in, and I cover up the blood with my duvet, then the door swings open and she

sees the screen and there's
this terrible long moment.

I close the laptop.

'Oh,' she says. 'Right.'

I finally stop talking and
I'm burning hot, like
overheating and

'Mark, love,' she says
quietly, 'is that two men?
On the screen?'

(*Barely able to speak*.) I
wanted to tell you, Mum…
this isn't how I wanted this
to happen.

For the first time in years,
he breaks down and cries.

(*As Dad*.) 'I'm not having
you wandering about,
doing that Darren. I'm not
having it.'

He gets up. Grabs his
keys.

(*As Dad*.) 'You're not
going to see him again, that
boy, okay? You're not
going school. I'll find you
a new school, yeah? /
I swear.'

Darren's dad leaves,
slamming the door.

My mum promises me that
she loves me and
everything will work itself
out. And amazingly, for the
first time in years, when
she tells me it's going to be
okay, I believe her.

And I hear him lock it from
the outside. He's fucking
locked me in.

DARREN *goes crazy,*
trying to get out, smashing

*and kicking and breaking
stuff in the flat. When he
realises he can't get out he
curls up in the middle of
the floor, surrounded by
white noise.*

She's laughing and I say
why are you laughing and
she says that she already
knew. She knew all along
because she's my mum and
of course she knew.

He tries to call MARK *but
he doesn't pick up.*

Dad finally comes back
and he's sees what I've
done to the flat / and...

(*As Dad.*) ...'The fuck
have you done Darren?'
And I look around and I
have fucking destroyed it.
Everything, all of it. (*As
Dad.*) 'Why'd you do this
Darren? You're so fucking
stupid.'

And he comes at me
swinging, and even though
I can see there's tears in his
eyes, he beats the shit out
of me.

MARK *curls up in a ball,
happy.*

DARREN *is on the floor
getting beaten.*

And then he's gone but
he's not locked the door
this time and I know I have
to get out.
I can't be at home
I can't be in school
I can't be in Brentford.

The next day, I pick up my
phone and I see I have a

missed call from Darren. I type a message to him... and then delete it.

I put my stuff in a bag and I get Mac and Cheese and head out with no plan. I sit in the playground with my hood up like a lump in the dark, bruises rising like my skin might burst.

And I'm so tired suddenly. Tired to my bones. I try to think but I'm – (*Hitting himself.*) too fucking stupid.

I type and delete and type and delete and delete and lock because there's only one thing I want to say and I can't say it.

He turns away.

And I realise there's only one place I can go.

So I go.

He circles the stage and arrives at...

Twenty

...MARK*'s house.*

MARK. I don't need to text him. I'll just see him at school. The wound is healing and I'm not... I'll just... go to school. It'll be fine.

Won't it?

Mum shouts up the stairs that she's heading out for Zumba.

She leaves and almost immediately there's a knock at the door.

Barney starts barking.

Barney shh. Stay. Forgot her phone probably.

I go downstairs and open the door, and…

It's DARREN. *His face is bruised and his lip is split and he has a large backpack.*

DARREN *puts on a bizarrely happy act, incongruent with the way he looks.*

DARREN. Hello mate.

,

Thought I'd pop round.

He steps through the door without being invited to.

,

Shall I take off my shoes?

He takes off his shoes, and pushes past MARK, *into the house.*

MARK *is on edge.* DARREN*'s in now and he can't get him out.*

MARK. What happened to your face?

DARREN. Nothing.

,

Is this okay? That I'm here?

,

Are you scared of me?

MARK *thinks for a moment but the truth is –*

MARK. No.

,

DARREN. Let's go upstairs.

DARREN *leads* MARK *up to his own bedroom.*

,

In the bedroom, neither of them speak for a while. Then at the same time:

DARREN. I'm really sorry.   MARK. Are you okay?
Not really.   It's okay. It's healing…

MARK. Did you get in a fight?

DARREN. Sort of.

MARK. What's with the bag? You moving in?

DARREN *shakes his head.*

DARREN. Just wanted to see you.

This lands softly on MARK. *He leans almost imperceptibly closer to* DARREN.

I was just thinking something…

MARK. What?

DARREN. I was wondering… do you love me?

,

Do you?

MARK. Yes. Yeah.

(*Aside.*) I say it even before I've thought about it, and I realise that despite everything,

it's true.

DARREN. Prove it.

MARK. I've missed you. I was going / to text but

DARREN. Fucking prove it Mark.

MARK *doesn't know what to do.*

DARREN *kisses him roughly.*

MARK. What you doing?

DARREN. Do you like that? Is this what fags like?

MARK. Don't call me that.

DARREN. You're bent Mark. It's dirty.

MARK. Darren, what's going on?

DARREN. My life has gone to shit, Mark. And it's your fucking fault.

MARK. No it's not.

DARREN. My dad locked me in the flat.

MARK. That's… that's not my fault Darren.

DARREN. My life has gone to complete shit.

MARK. It was shit anyway.

,

DARREN (*sotto*). Fuck you, man.

DARREN *lights a cigarette.*

MARK. Could you not smoke in here.

DARREN *continues to smoke.*

Darren.

Are you deaf?

Could you put that out?

DARREN. Got an ashtray?

MARK. No.

DARREN *continues to smoke, then holds out his arm and stubs the cigarette out on himself. It hurts. He grimaces.*

Darren, stop!

MARK *goes towards* DARREN, *who pushes him away. He burns himself again with the cigarette.*

Stop it! What's wrong with you?

DARREN *looks at the burns on his arm.*

DARREN. You think there's something wrong with me?

MARK. Just stop doing that.

MARK takes the cigarette from him and chucks it out the window.

DARREN. I fink you're right innit. I fink there is something wrong with me.

,

Will you help me Mark?

,

Will you?

MARK. Yeah. Yeah of course I will. It's going to be okay.

DARREN. I want you to do something for me. I want you to make me come.

MARK. What?

DARREN. Just an experiment, just a test. Come on.

MARK. No, I don't want to.

DARREN. Yes you do. Just this one little fing. You're fucking desperate for it.

MARK. No. Not like this.

DARREN. You said you was gonna help me.

MARK. Not like this Darren. Could you... could you / leave

MARK tries to open the door, but DARREN forces him to his knees, against the wall.

(*Almost silently.*) Darren, you're angry, you're not thinking.

DARREN. Shut the fuck up Mark, you don't know me.

DARREN undoes his trousers and pushes his penis into MARK's mouth and holds him there.

,

,

DARREN *comes.* MARK *retches on the floor.*

A long silence while they recover. DARREN *does his trousers up.*

See? It's dirty Mark. You don't love me.

DARREN *picks up his bag and leaves.*

MARK *stays on his hands and knees, heaving.*

Blackout.

Twenty-One

MARK *is still recovering, and slowly stands back up, unstable on his own feet. Café bell is sickening.*

MARK. In the café now. I watch the cogs turning slowly in his mind tick tick tick. 'If you don't have any A levels, tick tick tick, then what have you been doing all this time?'

Well. People can make their own prisons, Darren. You made one for me, remember? And I locked myself in it, getting more and more stoned, and I lost a lot of time, reliving and reliving. Even now. Even right now.

Mum was sympathetic at first, and then worried, and then frustrated, and then bored of me, bored of my empty life, so I got a job and moved out.

And here I am. Here we are.

Cogs turning slowly and that little free sample of joy feels very very far away. I can't stand here and celebrate his... his fresh fucking start.

I'm closed up and I'm reliving and he's kissing me and pushing me, that uninvited heat, that heart snap breaking. Reliving and reliving. It's not really living at all.

DARREN. Mark.

MARK *jumps slightly, startled out of his trauma.*

I missed you, man.

MARK (*inaudible*). What?

DARREN. I'm sorry.

MARK *shakes his head, so violently, that the scene crumbles away like an earthquake.*

Twenty-Two

MARK. Straight thin line and
I can't let it go.

DARREN. There's not a single
star and I can't go home.

There's a knock on MARK's bedroom door. He quickly straightens his shirt.

'Markie,' Mum says

Dad's on the sofa, amongst the mess and the broken… then, in a mumble, he goes,

'I've got a letter from school.'

'I've got a letter from school.'

School. Headteacher's office. MARK enters from one side. DARREN from the other.

MARK. I've been called into the head's office. I say to Mum that I don't want to go, but she says we have to go and she comes with me.

DARREN. I've got a meeting at school and my dad comes with me to make it look like he cares, but really it's coz he don't want me to see –

They see each other and stop. Neither knew the other was going to be here – this is the first time they've seen each other since the assault.

MARK (*turns to leave*). Fuck this.

DARREN (*sotto*). Shit.

MARK. No. I. Sorry miss I just can't. Be here.

,

(*Aside*.) My mum hisses in my ear to 'Sit. Down.' And I can't. Mum. I can't sit here.

Darren looks at his dad who nods once, silently, like a command, and they both sit down and I stay standing. It makes me feel weird and I realise I've never seen Darren… submit like that. He never does what people want him to do, he does the exact opposite and I stay standing. Darren looks ill, his bruises have yellowed and he looks thin and I stay standing. Darren stares at the ground but his dad stares right at me, assessing me, weighing me, and I wonder how much he knows and his eyes crush me until I realise,

I am actually sitting down.

DARREN. Why are we even here, miss? (*Sotto*.) Wasting my time man.

The headteacher snaps at him. They look up, scared, panic racing.

Sorry miss.

MARK (*aside*). Shit. Shit.

,

She knows.

Pointlessly, instinctively, MARK wipes his mouth. They listen to her, in fear, but their expressions change as, unexpectedly, she begins talking about the stolen bike.

DARREN. The bike, miss?

MARK. What bike?

DARREN. Yeah I actually can't even ride a bike, miss.

,

MARK (*aside*). She doesn't say anything, which is worse than when she was shouting.

Then my mum pipes up that I would never steal a bike. That I wouldn't even know how to steal a bike.

Then miss says there are 'eye witnesses'.

DARREN (*sotto*). Fucking snitch/es

MARK. Well I've been off sick miss, I haven't even been here, so...

DARREN. I did it miss. Mark was tryin' to stop me.

MARK *gives* DARREN *a look like 'what you doing?!'*

,

Nah he wasn't involved. I nicked the cutters. I cut the lock.

,

Mark wouldn't do that miss. He's got a bike at home. Ain't you Markie?

DARREN *addresses* MARK *for the first time and it stings.*

Ain't you Markie?

MARK (*sotto*). Yeah.

DARREN. You've got a really good bike at home, ain't you?

MARK (*sotto*). Yeah. I do.

,

(*Aside.*) But then she asks why I've missed so much school...

,

'He's not been well,' Mum says, but miss just keeps asking more and more questions and

DARREN. It's coz I pulled a knife on him, miss.

No one was expecting this.

MARK (*aside*). Mum's going, 'What?! What are you talking about?!' And Darren's dad puts his head in his hands and says 'Jesus fuck.'

,

What miss? No it's /

DARREN. Show 'er.

MARK. 'This is a very serious confession Darren,' she says.

DARREN. Show 'er!

> MARK *doesn't. He remains motionless, confused. Eventually* DARREN *reaches over and aggressively lifts* MARK*'s shirt, attempting to reveal the straight thin line that* DARREN *cut into him, but* MARK *jumps back.*

MARK. Don't fucking touch me.

> ,

DARREN. Fine.

> DARREN *gets up.*

> (*To headteacher.*) Nah miss. Don't want to fucking sit down.

> MARK *doesn't move, just looks at* DARREN.

MARK. Mum's shouting and pointing, 'How could the school let this happen?!' And Darren's dad is going 'You can't be fucking serious Darren.'

DARREN. I am fucking serious.

> So what?

> You gonna put me away? Coz I'm dangerous? Coz you're all fucking scared?

MARK. Darren.

DARREN (*sotto, smiling*). No. You're going to be stuck here alone bruv and I'm going to be free.

> ,

> That's what's gonna happen.

> MARK *stands there, realising he's finally lost* DARREN.

> Go on. Fuck off then.

> MARK *tumbles back to the café.*

Twenty-Three

Now.

MARK. This is my story and I've never told anyone before so. Don't interrupt.

Because I can't help it. I can't stop it playing again and again and again. Every piece. Every word.

DARREN. I missed you, man.

MARK. It's not really living at all.

DARREN. I'm sorry.

,

He reaches out to touch MARK's *hand, which is resting on the counter.*

MARK, *so shocked by this touch, does not immediately move away.*

After a moment, he does, and turns away.

Please Mark man. Just sit wiv me for five minutes. I want to make it up to you.

MARK (*sotto*). Don't touch me then.

,

DARREN. Mark, I was fifteen.

MARK. So was I.

DARREN. I had no clue what I was doing.

MARK. Neither did I.

DARREN. And I've been inside for four years Mark, I've been suffocating where no one knows me and you do. You know me. Just sit wiv me for five minutes.

Please. Five minutes. You're the only one.

MARK (*aside*). Something about him pleading... something about him acknowledging me, something about his hands,

that I've been wanting and missing, and even though I'm
going in fucking circles, it makes me forgive him and love
him so badly and I say…

fine.

Sit down and I'll, umm…

you want anything?

DARREN. Really? Mark. Thanks this is… yeah. I've… (*Digs
in his pockets.*) Haven't got my wallet though.

MARK *gestures that it's fine*.

Oh right. Right okay. Thanks.

MARK *smiles weakly*.

Thanks, well… umm bacon roll please.

MARK. Tea, coffee?

DARREN. Just black coffee. Thanks.

MARK *nods*.

DARREN *sits at a table*.

MARK. I go to the kitchen. I open the fridge. Bacon, loads of it.
Raw and pink. I throw three rashers onto the hot griddle. It
changes colour and I flip it and reach for a crusty roll. I cut
the roll through the middle and layer the bacon inside.

I'm about to grab the tomato sauce but then I stop because

who's in charge here, anyway? *I fink you're right innit. I fink
there is somefing wrong with me.* I suddenly see myself
standing there, making a bacon roll for the person who…
Will you help me Mark? Will you? The person who ripped up
my life. *Yeah of course, of course I'll help you. It's going to
be okay Darren.* I've never been with anyone else. I'll never
be with anyone else. I can't now… and no one should have
to do this. No one should have to stand in the same room
with the person who –

I have forgiven him and unforgiven him so many times and
I've loved him and I've hated him and I've needed him and

he wasn't there and I need to stop going in these fucking circles.

The memories are imprinted in my mind like ink that spreads and he got away like *You're going to be stuck here alone bruv and I'm going to be free*. And I'm still stuck. And I still love him. People make their own prisons Darren. You made one for me, remember?

And I'm at *work* and this is *my* story and the reason I'm telling you now is because

he's here

and who's in charge here, anyway?

I chuck the bacon roll into the food waste.

MARK *walks over to* DARREN.

DARREN. You gonna take off that apron at some point?

MARK. We're out of bacon.

DARREN. Ah no worries. Just the coffee is fine. I just wanted to –

MARK. We're out of coffee too.

MARK *holds his gaze.*

DARREN. Mark man, you won't even give me five minutes?

MARK (*tight, painful*). No. I can't do it.

DARREN. Mark, please. I'm sorry.

MARK (*shakes his head*). It has to be someone else.

,

It can't be me.

They hold each other's gaze.

Lightly, the bell above the door tinkles.

Blackout.

End.

A Nick Hern Book

Bacon first published in Great Britain in 2022 as a paperback original by Nick Hern Books Limited, The Glasshouse, 49a Goldhawk Road, London W12 8QP, in association with Finborough Theatre, London

Bacon copyright © 2022 Sophie Swithinbank

Sophie Swithinbank has asserted her moral right to be identified as the author of this work

Cover image: Alex Britt and Sam Craig, photographed by Darius Shu

Designed and typeset by Nick Hern Books, London
Printed in the UK by Mimeo Ltd, Huntingdon, Cambridgeshire PE29 6XX

A CIP catalogue record for this book is available from the British Library

ISBN 978 1 83904 075 7

Woodland
CARBON
www.woodlandcarbon.co.uk
NICK HERN BOOKS
Printed on Carbon Captured paper

www.nickhernbooks.co.uk

facebook.com/nickhernbooks

twitter.com/nickhernbooks